Infertile Bliss, Infertile Woe: A Poetry Chapbook in Yoga Sequence

Lara Diallo

BookLeaf Publishing

Presentation by *BookLeaf Publishing*

Web: www.bookleafpub.com

E-mail: info@bookleafpub.com

ISBN: 9789357210720

First edition 2022

DEDICATION

To the greatest of all my God-given blessings:
Nene-Bella, Alpha, and Rhea

PREFACE

If I could sum up in three words what I, as a woman, needed to hear at every turning point in my life, it is this: You are enough. My hope is that you will own these words for yourself. My prayer is that life feels more at ease when you do.

Uneasy Seat

Trying to find ease,
Straining, mind racing, forgetting
The golden key: breathe…

Infertile Bliss

Child (playing outside my window) less
room as I inhale another
cup of mo(u)rning menstrual tea
blood between my lips, the
bar (stool seeps red yet) ren
-dered infertile bliss.
Wondering what I have to miss.

Infertile Woe

they said we were blocked,
they said we were slow,
they, sullen-faced, deepened our woe.
    You would be mocked.

    so, we worked as we waited,
we split meals for breakfast,
we ran races for lunch,
we surrendered the wine and sacrificed our daily bread.

we bettered ourselves like a pair of eagles swooping
    in, calculating their dinner.

You, the wind, sweeping through the upper room.

no rest of the weary,
no play for the tired and worn,
no hug for the teary,
no time to mourn,
    as we sit on the toilet,
    watching the stick.

all of our toil, vainly reading negative.
    just a big, fat 0, not +, nor -.

but not by works of righteousness (which we have),
but according to (Your) mercy,
but Your love spreading thick
    covering even the crusts of our daily bread.

there we were -
waiting as we wait -
for the doc to give the okay -
for me to go under and -
maybe just maybe we'd understand the why -
to all this waiting -

3 tedious years toppling like a Jenga game,
3 tedious miles we drove to the hospital,
3 tedious minutes before the anesthesia,
3 light-shifting words that made faith be sight.
    we took off our glasses to see,
    really see there were

4 of us in the fire.
    You, giver of 3 babies later.

To Lift My Face

To lift my face,
to lift the burden I carry,
it would take some massive strength,
yet I simply sit passive at length.

Hells below and heavens above and I trudge
upon dust,
Questioning if I can live like this,
Contemplating one more day or even if
I can but must-
er the strength.

To lift my face,
to lift the burden I carry,
waiting 4 a miracle
that hasn't arrived in
time,
waiting 4 an arrival
to save time
4

To lift my face,
to lift the burden I carry,
eyes closed, mouth strained,
doors closed, groping for an opportunity pane.

None I see,
though there be
1.

Mountain Pose

Strong gaze, power legs
Firming, force-filled fired up form,
My Tadasana.

The Natural Birthing Experience

It was hell. Shots firing from
all cylinders, my anxious helpers. The Ring
of Fire was grounding, pulling, total in
of body experience.
Dripping edges of sanity playing in
and out my mind. Making me
feel like a lousy lady in
line at Lowe's complaining.
Too many nosy eyes, too many strangers' sighs
The heat bubbling over and out
The kitchen stove pot putters I can'ts, I won'ts, I
don'ts,
I wonder why we're not being listened to
But you stuck it out with me through and to
Break through
Your needs elevating mine
Desperate for mommy, Father, anybody to see with
hearing eyes
"Why, oh, why?" We
cry,
heave,
sigh,
breathe.

The Unnatural Birthing ExperienCe

It was heaven. UnsCrupulous legs tingling, heavy.
The Breath of Life was lifting, freeing,
Total out of body experience.
Distant voiCes and faCes.
Ethereal feeling fading
of surroundings.   Then,
stabbing knives begin to priCk
me in the front like a true friend would.
The betrayal of it all.   My Paradise Lost.

I Know When I See You I Am

I know when I leave the room
  you'll cry just like
I know when I come near
  you'll smile just like
I know when I give you milk
  you'll rest with ease just like

When I see you, I am happy.
When I see you, I am accepted.
When I see you, I am content.

When I see you, I am filled with the entirety of the universe,
every speck of dust that exists is spiraling all around us
like confetti at a birthday party.

When I hold you, this universe explodes within and
I am become love.

Child's Pose

Take a bow inward
Supple body guarding heart
I surrender all

Her Pink Princess Shoes

Where is she going in those heels of hers?
Trapesing across the room, arms dancing,
smile spread like a watercolor painting.
The colors flow out of her silk dress:
light blues when I send her up for a nap,
purple hues when she comes over for a hug, so snug,
green spews when we gather our hands, clasped,
circling
round and round until we fall down.

With a few more pixie steps, she stands on her tip
toes
and more colors leave drip drops:
a gray splatch,
some blackness,
yellow,
orange,
brown,
all come colliding down.

A rainbow of light encircles her steps and guides
me to her evanescence,
leaving me to awe at this wonderful kaleidoscope
God gave me,
a promise of hope when all is said and done.

Her heels are placed high in the closet for
the next special time when she gets to become
the rainbow she was always meant to be for me.

Mother's Piano

The sound of the black and white keys
danc ing in stac ca to set a

tiny
match
burning,
ever so brighter,
as I snuggled under
my blanket, on that cushy
sofa, and leaned my head against
the cool leather, warming it up by the
friction of war and peace and peace and war.

Then (inhaling that vanilla candle),

the notes languorously moved together as she
held the right pedal down for four measures oh
the happy, the peace, the joy, the bright time of
this house when my sister and I ran endlessly
around and around and around the fireplace of
our childhood.

I Remember

I remember being pulled out of bed
in the middle of the night. It was still
so dark outside. I grip the sheets as fear covers
me.
Had I done something wrong?

I wish I knew
how to undo
what I had done so
as not to incur the fury of my Grandmother's woe
or the downcast look from my mother's face as
she withdrew.

Grandma was ripping off my bed sheets,
my eyes now opened fully, but my head retained
fuzzy
and I, sleepy, weary, cold, was in the wrong
and started to cry. I cried out of being scared
and fearful and feeling judgment cover
me with one evil, eye-piecing glance.
That scowl. I would feel that scowl for the rest of
my life,
whenever I naively made an error or in my innocence
and ignorance did something deemed foolish
and ignorant.

Funny, even after I washed my sheets
and was pushed back towards my bedroom did I
only then
realize that my clothes were asking to be changed
because they retained water.
Grandma said I had wet
the bed, so the wet
must be from that, but for a moment ---

I simply thought it was from the
water as we washed the sheets
in the downstairs marble bathtub. And I,
just an innocent who had incurred the wrath of
judgment's inscrutable hand
that was meant for someone else,
not me, innocent me.

Tree Pose

One foot down to ground,
One leg bent aright, to be
A community.

The Christmas Table Runner

A black and red plaid runs slainfully
upon the wooden dining room table
as the instant coffee aroma rises.

The gingerbread cookies brown in the oven,
a small sacrifice for hangry children.
Oh that cozywarmand feeling
that begins near the end of the Eve of Christmas.

Burnt offerings placed on the table covering,
the splattering of red
and gristle of blackened ash.

Born again like a baptism by fire and blood.
A mother's birthing cry like a frog in a boiling
pot -
I sit, not shaken, unstirred, a crematorium after
the burn.
The Angel of Death arrives with a sinister smile.

I burn, I boil, unassuming,
enthroned in the swaddling cloth
upon the alter of thy sin.

Pulling Roots

Tall sky rising sighs
Emptiness in fullness bloom
You without the me

Robin kneels to pray
Fullness in wilting flower
Me without the you

Us pulling up roots
Like gory entrails waving
"Goodbye! So Long!" Gone.

The Bonsai Tree

The bonsai tree stands erect on the nightstand
by that open window where the moon peaks in
on cloudless nights.

I sit in easy seat on the floor
upon that red Arabian nights rug ready to fly me
to samadhi
on this particular cloudless night.

And there lies the Holy Bible beside me,
pages turning my mind open to love
on this particular cloudless night.

I meditate the incensed air.
I meditate the burning bonsai tree.
I meditate the full bright moon.

And sitting there, I verily, verily meet the
Trinity,
and mitigate the love that rushes over me,
like a deluge.

The Warrior Series

Test one, square your hips
Sink down and lengthen your way
To upward salute

Test two, energize
Stabilize and breathe deeply
Fierce focus to peace

Test three, sacrifice
Humbling balance slicing night
Shoot my energy

Fearful ego flees
When determination leads
Grace to heart center

War Seal

There was a war seal
on the letter you sent me
so many moons ago.

It was red, splotched, rained on, static, silly oh
me made me think of silly oh us.

I marooned over the time spent,
I in regret, us worlds apart,
oceans and hearts.

You see, that wax seal has never been slit open.

I wonder what you said so many moons ago.
There lies a wax seal on the letter you sent me
in corpse pose.

Namaste.

Corpse Pose

To stare death face up,
In-exhale, mastering breath,
Calm, acceptance, rest.

www.ingramcontent.com/pod-product-compliance
Lightning Source LLC
Chambersburg PA
CBHW051717130826
49812CB00034B/1230
* 9 7 8 9 3 5 7 2 1 0 7 2 0 *